Summer Snow

By the same author

Alibi (pamphlet)

R4,200g DIDiscs.
(pron. _Pardle_.)

SUMMER SNOW

Ruth Padel

HUTCHINSON
London Sydney Auckland Johannesburg

© Ruth Padel 1990

The right of Ruth Padel to be identified as author of this work
has been asserted by Ruth Padel in accordance with the
Copyright, Designs and Patent Act, 1988

This edition first published in 1990 by *(100 DL advance*
Hutchinson *(£ 64 royalties)*

Century Hutchinson Ltd, 20 Vauxhall Bridge Road, London
SW1V 2SA

Century Hutchinson Australia (Pty) Ltd
20 Alfred Street, Milsoms Point, Sydney, NSW 2061

Century Hutchinson New Zealand Limited
PO Box 40–086, Glenfield, Auckland 10, New Zealand

Century Hutchinson South Africa (Pty) Ltd
PO Box 337, Bergvlei, 2012 South Africa

British Library Cataloguing in Publication Data
Padel, Ruth 1946–
Summer snow.
I. Title
823'.914

ISBN 0–09–174285–4

Set in Times by Input Typesetting Ltd, London
Printed and bound in Great Britain
by Cox and Wyman, Reading

out to be a long association with Oxford when she went up in 1965 to read classics at Lady Margaret Hall. Her doctoral thesis on the idea of the mind in Greek tragedy took seven years to complete; time she divided between trips to Crete, where she picked up modern Greek, and stints of teaching in Oxford. Her loyalty and affection for the place stem from this time: Wadham College made her its first female fellow, changing its statutes to accommodate her. The 1970s marked the beginning of the great revolution in classical studies: Oxford was in the thick of it, and Padel was in her element. "It was just when structuralism was coming to the fore – a very heady time, intellectually," she recalls. "And that freedom spilled over into the rest of life. I lived for a while with the sculptor Michael Black. He taught me how to live a creative life: when he needed money, he made prints and sold them. That's the model on which I still operate."

She left Oxford in 1976 and returned to Crete, teaching English while she whittled her thesis into a book. And it was here that she began, tentatively, to write the poems that would eventually appear in her first collection – though publication remained over a decade off. Back in London, she took a teaching post at Birkbeck and met and married Myles Burnyeat, professor of ancient philosophy at Cambridge. In 1985, their daughter, Gwen, was born, and the event acted as an unexpected catalyst for Padel's writing.

"Everything had been gradually amassing, but Gwen's arrival seemed to open the gates," she says, "because of the focus it brought." She published her first pamphlet of poems, *Alibi*, that year, and slowly set about establishing herself as a freelance writer, despite finding that, in journalism, "poetry isn't a great calling-card. I know of one editor who said: 'I'd never have anything to do with a poet; they never say what they mean.' So I felt I wasn't seen as a very good bet, but I gradually found a niche for myself."

As the writing took off, however, Padel returned to London with her daughter (then five). The family saw one another at weekends, but distance took its toll; Burnyeat and Padel eventually separated, "although we remain very good friends". Her first full-length collection, *Summer Snow*, came out in 1990, when she was 44, and the inclusion of a poem from it in a PEN anthology led to an encounter with another poet, Matthew Sweeney, that had a profound effect on her career. At a party for the anthology, Sweeney invited her to take part in his workshop, whose membership (Don Paterson, Sean O'Brien, Jo Shapcott, Michael Donaghy, Lavinia Greenlaw and Sarah Maguire, among others) reads like the roll-call of a generation.

"It was," she acknowledges now, "a movement, or something like it. We'd meet once a month at the Lamb pub on Conduit Street, bringing a poem each and considering them anonymously. My second collection, *Angel*, came out of the surprisingness of that process. Matthew had a genius for diagnosing a poem: he wouldn't say how to fix it, but he'd put his finger on the sore spot. It was he, too, who led to the formal shift in my work that happened in [the 1998 collection] *Rembrandt Would Have Loved You*. I was complaining about not being able to get away from three-liners, and he said: 'Well, you're stuck on it! Do something completely different.' So I started writing these big, structured poems, full of capitals and indentations – fantastically artificial-seeming things, but I found they imposed a wonderful formality. I became obsessed with this idea of form as a means of moving through the tangle."

Padel won the National Poetry competition in 1997 with "Icicles Round a Tree in Dumfriesshire", the opening poem of *Rembrandt Would Have Loved*

Mal Peet finds some wonderfully nasty creations in Chris Wooding's latest novel

Malice

by Chris Wooding
384pp, Scholastic, £6.99

In 2007, Scholastic published *The Invention of Hugo Cabret*, a brilliantly innovative book written and drawn by Brian Selznick, in which the narrative is part prose, part beautifully cinematic sequences of monochrome drawings. Perhaps inspired by Selznick, Chris Wooding's *Malice* (the first in a series from the same publisher) contains episodes in the form of pages from a graphic novel. The book's premise is excellent. It's *Malice Through the Looking-Glass*, a Goth-horror update of Lewis Carroll.

Teenagers are becoming poisonously obsessed by a very nasty cult comic called Malice. Some of them enact rituals that physically transport them into its world, where they meet – or narrowly evade – ends that are very gruesome indeed. As one would expect from a writer as darkly inventive as Wooding, the world of Malice is full of wonderfully nasty creations. The Chitters are dagger-clawed, mechanical horrors that kill by sucking time out of their victims.

I confess that I didn't take to the central characters, Seth, Justin and Kady. Plunged into the nightmare of Malice, these teenagers (who in the real world are troubled in their different ways) morph into junior versions of Rambo, *Die Hard*'s John McClane and Lara Croft – especially in the graphic sections. Confronted by unimaginable horrors, they lapse into the cheesily laconic, wisecracking dialogue of the action hero. Although only Kady is American, they all start to use American movie-speak and mannerisms. This may be knowing and witty. These kids have been translated into a comic, so they become two-dimensional, right? Maybe. Or maybe Wooding has at least one eye on the US market. Either way, I found it irritating and unconvincing. The challenge of fantasy writing is to make it real. Wooding can do this, as he showed in the excellent *Storm Thief*. In *Malice*, he tells us (frequently) that his characters are "scared, really scared", but their joshing camaraderie contradicts it.

One of the interesting effects of the hybridity of both *Hugo Cabret* and *Malice* is that it obliges the reader to switch between two modes of reading. Reading the prose, we picture things in our heads. Reading the pictures, we supply most of the words. Shifting back and forth between the two is demanding, which is fine. It's also fun. But reading graphics is slower and more complicated than reading prose, so alternating the two involves taking considerable risks with pace and tension. And *Malice* doesn't always get away with it.

To be fair, it's very hard for an illustrator (in this case, Dan Chernett) to depict huge, monstrous events in a series of black-and-white panels squeezed on to a page the size of an ordinary paperback. It's unfortunate, though, that some of Wooding's grisly imaginings become merely silly in the drawings. Ironically (or perhaps encouragingly) the prose is more visual than the pictures. But these are an old man's quibbles. Young teenagers, for whom the book is intended and who are more attuned to the conventions of the games console, are far more likely to be swept along by Wooding's restless, relentless imagination. And to wait impatiently for the next volume.

Mal Peet's latest novel is *Exposure* (Walker). To order *Malice* for £6.99 with free UK p&p call Guardian book service on 0330 333 6846 or go to gaurdian. co.uk/bookshop

For Elaine Feinstein

Acknowledgements

The author and publishers wish to thank the following magazines and collections where some of these poems have appeared: *PN Review*, *Kenyon Review*, *Numbers*, *Pequod*, *Alibi: Pamphlet of poems by Ruth Padel* (The Many Press, 1985), *PEN Anthology III* (1988), National Poetry Competition *Prizewinners' Anthology* 1985, Ver Poets Poetry Competition *Prizewinners' Anthology* 1989.

Contents

8

PART ONE

The Earliest Map

Two hundred dry miles north of Babylon
they found the earliest map.
A delta. One river through it,
four or five thousand
years ago inscribed
on a small clay leaf.

This neat obedient man
sitting beside me on the hot night train
to Larissa, traces Greek football pools
on yellow paper. What else is there?
We transfer space evasively,
hide in the yellow spice of the acacia,

routes by which we came
untraceable, except the stigmata
of educator, doctor, rail time-table.
We live Babylonian hours, minutes, space.
Their 'three hundred and sixty'
enfolds us. Their river

veins through to our end:
this shanty littoral,
a wishful, forgetting mind
penned on a dry clay leaf.

Shards

Why does the private matter?
Oleanders
ice-cream colours
ruff the smart new roads.

*

Language from the well.
Decipherment
has broken in our mouths.
Eagles leave,
calling on the sun
to dry their wings.

*

Dun goats, a frieze
of blue and bronze and gold.
. . . tiny arum lily's
green-white trumpet curled
round a single pistil
in the last light on Ida.

*

Copper replaces iron.
Pain we don't remember
leaves its mark. Where is the sound
in the song?

*

. . . draught-board of lapis lazuli:
war-games. Scarabs, seals
overlain
by Saracen coin.

*

Who could foresee
horizons of destruction
so complete?
Mute burnt levels . . .

*

Our sandals fill with seeds.

Herodotus in Egypt Remembers Delos

The ground verdigris, fluffy with young mosquitoes. Waters
sacred as these, as fatted with reeds. Bronze palm planted
to Sun. Lizards, Nile alligators, hindquarters
rolling on granite sphinx-chippings. Air salted with confident
brown larks. Travelling, you remember (mind
upturning these foreign priests, finding
the causes) that stamen-summit: white long
unbloody altar, giddy blues under you, calyx of bronze
flat islands unfolding, blind.

Betrayal

Above the sea I found two mules
tethered by the leg to a thornbush
in blue-fire sky. Their shared bell
outrang the small white sanctuary below.
I brought away a long smooth ilex acorn.
My interior Cyprus, reached only now
by the travellator's depthless Styx,
dreams through me on return

in the overheated airport bus
through backstreets blossoming with nylon curtains
like the ones I've seen in army lemon gardens,
puffed by exhaust of English hoovers
sucking Dralon-buttoned sofas, blowing
soft white tears, a set for *Così Fan Tutte,*

over English toothpaste from the NAAFI,
while Turkish planes raped giant orange groves,
following their Sultan
after four hundred and fifty years.
I pass into blue denim cloud,
a grey fringed fen, a null horizon
like a drying wound, a British sunset's
guilty roseate skull.

Exorcism
(for my brother Felix)

(i)
Window seat

First snow. Silverhazel on rough grass.
Apocryphal garden, green jade
of the Duc de Berry's Hours
against the greenblack yew.
An aching landscape late in the century
reached by a fat blue gate.

Everywhere else the English day
was black-edged, unlearnable,
a joined-up mystery
all the way to school.
Where does darkness come from?
It was years before the names arose

and called her. Not till she'd learned
a grammar of elsewhere:
confidence off the map,
where sea glittered with plastic bags
and jellyfish in opulent morning,
and suckers of raw octopus burned all night,

where roads had no proper edge
for deep disorder runs
radiant and disobedient over all.
Some sudden sorcery of remembering
lifted the reliquary's lid.
Imprisoned lights crept out

16

with halitus of mothballs,
peatsmoke, the grand piano's
ivory breath, an English physiology
of tea-times, uncles, words:
magnets sunk before the world grew up
in a mind that failed

to learn its proper place.
Discovering Minoan script
she saw home landscapes fall
into order on a hazelpath,
a velvet caravan of compost heaps,
reached by a rotting gate.

(ii)
Childhood is feudal

'Have you consulted
enchanters and magicians,
have you made vows
to trees and fountains
have you drunk
any magic philtres?'
Well, yes – I have.
Last time my cow was sick.

Through medicinal months,
their village names –
Springmonth, Joymonth,
Ploughmonth, Windmonth,
Vintagemonth, Holymonth –
you stared at phoenix-skins:
vermilion feathersticks
at St Denys' Fair.

What you've lost defines you.
Light that matters on the stage
casts shadow. Spells
the bee-master laid on you
long ago, tatty and potent
as a Christmas robin
in an oriental city's winter yard,
now work their way to the wind.

(iii)
Hibernation

Hoarding the vintage, turn
where you learned to trust. Within.
Let stem-sinews burn outside
and the tidy trellis rust.
Paint, clip, glove your vine alone.
This harvest bleeds when cut.
Winter sleep sweetens
and darkens taciturn dust.
Oiled feathers tickle the cellar lock.
Shadows you don't expect
grunt up from granite fern.

(iv)
Home ground

Then let go and be consumed by the cool.
This is in the things and shines in the things.
(Christopher Middleton)

The Boeing-bird, a dotty silver omen,
beady as the jerfalcon,
    arctic acrobat
    bought with oil
        and smuggled
        under the backseat
    of a Vauxhall Viva,
    dowry for the daughter
of a sheik, illegal survivor
from a sandy sky, now brings us back

to *broderie anglaise.*
To Heathrow environs,
    flat green in soggy evening,
    birthmarked by cables.
        Lights climb the night
        as we go down, a fiery mouth
    of orange-peel,
    aromatic edges in the pyre
of a night land
left behind.

(v)
Grandchild

Medusa kiss of Christmas fog
tickles the running car.
Someone is watching you from furred bridges
whose trembling concrete hessian
flashes lemon and rose-madder
in a spray of wet sunset,
crumbling suddenly
to a screen of Egyptian dusk.

A motorway-throatful
of padded interiors beat
behind foreign names. Opel,
Mercedes, Citroën, Volkswagen,
Honda – floating fires
as lonely as the Ganges,
surprisingly fatal companions –
discolour in rainy twilight

subsiding to muslin mist
like lips touching alcohol,
on B-roads left behind.
Fudge-brown clouds. Sky –
just a black ending
to the city's orange breath –
spreads italic memory on English grass:

a ragged film for frowsty
front-room walls, smudged
as the Gainsborough sketch
of a sleeping child, on the stairs.
Tall silent rooms,
an alphabet of adult light,
chocolate with an eternal
mothball taste, kept in the drawer

with wool left from seventeen
grandchildren's jerseys.
Peatblocks, mossy heavy heaps,
propped the schoolroom fire.
Rooms with élitist names.
Somewhere midnight stands at the door
of a child who can't sleep
till a private iridescent grammar

studs dawn grass, and brownsilver leaves
float up from the witch-dark path.
This house is waiting.
Every nativity is hurt.

Small Painting

He made it for me long after,
on a cigar-box lid. Navy sky.
Colours weren't real without black,
he said. But a horizontal silvery scratch
lets blue rays fall to a rough trail,
moonshine on sea. You can't tell
if it's mountain beyond or cloud
but I think – or maybe remember,
it's so long ago and there's only this –
it's a hill. From my window
hill filled the eyes. We climbed
in a drizzly mud haze.
I saw my first bog asphodel.
No cairn, no proper top.

I took this off the wall
after driving up the motorway alone
last night, thinking of your 'unlivable'.
This is your sea. I can hold it.
Is your hill somewhere close by?

The Tarot-Reader's Daughter

There are places where he says home.
They don't satisfy but they're his work.
Even temptations start in the living-room
under the light by the goldfish.

When she says it, places come and go
she never thought of while she stayed.
A slope of vicious sun, quick jokes,
could have housed her. Somehow she left.

A city where you might think you'd be safe.
Down buttery anti-parking lines,
the smoothest curve in Europe,
pad shades of men who loved

and were kept distant by her,
some now dead. She melted
to other people's myths. Went away.
Leaving was part of her gift.

Childhood was surface panicked over,
no mug without its saucer,
hidden things interpreted too easily,
brought out to doctors and guests

at the drop of invisible hats.
Children bringing stories,
confusing love and present,
met decipherment instead.

Having dismantled dwellings everywhere
she lives in going between,
always where she's not, imagining
she might be known some night.
Or if not known, divined. Throwing out
entrails, knowing was never enough.

Explaining the North Yorkshire Afghan Hounds Rescue Association

We buy because they'll look glamorous
plus we can cuddle them now.
We think vaguely of gazelles,
pre-Iran Persia; Bardot. Not of legs
that despise boundaries, shit
(a monthly twelve-pound yield –
it must go somewhere), or wet
domestic trust. Teeth that turn combs,
interior flora alien to ours,
a mania for things' insides, expensive
wine-glasses shattered by tail.
If we don't spend the first year training them
to be immobile though they're made to run,
to sit and sleep alone, fetch love
the way we want, we take the motorway
and dump them on the moor. Someone
will pick up this tab. Needy as women, vicious –
not up to us to sort these tangles out.

Byzantium Remembers Waiting

Sea-discoverers went to other worlds.
Vagabond eyes ignored my site
in a goldenfleece sea. Dry here, blank,
a snowdrop-travesty of morning, I waited.
My sea-crocus, shore-froth,
wild pale plumbago and convolvulus,
watched colonists moving in at Chalcedon
whose northeast current pushes every boat away.

I waited another thirty years. Shy
dazzle of candid mist, self-doubtful
as a mirage, I received
September migrants. Cranes cried,
shelling my rain. I grounded the night heron's
looped throat in purple reeds, in love
with birds of prey and passage. Now,
strand-marked by Byzas, sperm-spread silk

on a rising sea, I harden into chronicle.
Fire stares from my helmet-roofs,
heart-splitting skyline, my bridges,
gazelles, modestly dancing bears.
Divinities and legions stir in me.
Stiff-skirted politicians launch
libraries of retrospect. My ships will travel
in arrears, to crypts beyond this sun.

Siege
(for E.R. Dodds)

All I could do was find more blankets for him,
    tell how the fighting went
    at the walls he'd often painted,
    carcass-plumed by now in violet smoke.
    He'd loved our city in its land.
    Seeing the things he'd made
    you couldn't help loving it his way:
    a blue remote unfleshly background.
    You'd hardly think this was the place
    we worked and died and were afraid in.
    You knew it was. But different.
    Tenderer. More important.

I gave him, and the others,
    fingering self-fragments
    in the arrowy shadow,
    touching and a name.
    We never drive the swallows out.
    I don't know why they like it,
    our hall of frightened warriors
    (flies poach their sticky sweetness),
    rotting in stale
    sunlight trapped by stone.
    If our walls do break
    each one will cry to me

to have his throat cut first.
    Redgold beakers, crust-coated blankets,
    spittle in sun. Grim unreadable stars
    hold his eyes. They are all
    forbidden to complain.

Hope falls from all of us
leaving a vein of white. The summer months
go by. Palm Sunday last
he finished his Annunciation,
then caught his sickness at the end of May.
Rainbows fell between the altar doors
when we nailed his ikon up. A dark girl

masked and nipped by lilies.
   Dark green shadows. One stiff hand out
   trying to say, No. Sun
   through their ears and nails,
   hair the soft same colour on both sides,
   something that joined them. Bare.
   A puzzled angel brought up short
   by this dashboard of a madonna
   packed in silver. Shy quills of light
   like water on her sleeve,
   on the angel's fingers,
   on the air where their eyes meet.

Now he's unmaking all he did
   and questioning. 'Should Judas
   be older than your Christ?
   The virgin than the angel?
   Painting is rediscovering a meeting.
   I could re-do your ikon,
   make the girl *enceinte* with flowers
   of satin only. Plumstain velvet. I see it now:
   a warm, round, manmade shell,
   protected by nothing natural.
   Or hidden in a ruined purple garden
   layered with bryony, insects, regret.

29

'Her hand still out, though, warding off
        the stranger. He hangs on the day
        like dust, lifts random light
        higher . . . a little higher . . .
        before the quick night comes.'
Mad freckling, rich geometry
of difficult relationships,
moments of lone pain. Whorls
of delirium: the painter's occupations.
He clings to my arm like soot.
The island's afternoon
whirrs stickily to dusk.

'That's how I'd do it! Look!
        A stumbling Christ! White blistered thumb
        above the cross. Pull into centre,
        secretly – you'd have to search for them –
        His bloodclot of black mourners
        on a tiny khaki hill. Then the eyes should wind,
        a plumbline tangled, following the woolly crowd –
        a sailor bends for a snapping buckle, waggons
        swarm with children – till you see,
        centre again but very small,
        Christ slip on a rock. Chestnut fold
        of hair across His eye.

'Chestnut again the back of His hand,
        repeated in woodgrain on the cross.
        Flat cloud like asterblossom
        as a soldier sees dawn fog
        through battlements like tears.
        Are they brush-strokes on His shoulder
        or stripes of yellow pain?
        Lying here – this *paliasse* in your corner
        under torse-moulded capitals –

reminds me of the north. The past.
I am a weathervane
of image and memory now.

Eagles in western mountains,
    snow on the wing. Barn owls
    near Bayeux, hunting: their round,
    surprised-seal faces
    through early summer night.
    Bitter curling leaves,
    tow-coloured wind on an empty hillside,
    pomegranate trees, red-dotted
    in battle-order. Thyme-lawns
    with their cloak of orange bees.
    But you – you didn't come here
    to learn these things.'

No. I'm a stranger too. My home also
    was in the north and west.
    I go on saying daily,
    'Useless to amputate. Dead
    within the hour,' examining
    fresh seeds of shell in greening flesh,
    ripped bulblets of cell-fabric,
    soft crucibles of pain.
    Everything unmade. Eyes'
    red yolk down a cheek, guts unravelling
    glaucous un-named weed. My friend
    who left this morning for the walls –

beige and slashed green velvet, sleek
    confident French scent and sunlight
    on a new-bought handkerchief –
    they brought him in at noon,
    a slime of leaping meat

on drying board. All my learning
useless: Galen and the Coan Treatises,
comfrey learned and picked
in northern woods.
I didn't come here to learn these things,
knowledge that's a mess
to have to know.

The painter has a canker in his throat.
He keeps swallowing on nothing. Says
his mouth feels dry. Afraid of choking most,
he keeps asking of the siege outside,
beguiled, professionally, by artifice.
I gossip. The new defence from Venice:
our men are digging tunnels at right angles
to the Turk below our walls. They stretch
across them membranes sewn with bells.
These shiver, jump in the city's throat,
shake a little thunderstorm of dust-chimes
when the infidels are down there, laying shells.

The blast will ray out, weakened, and our walls
are saved. You see? Do you understand?
Hidden corridors in bowels of our city . . .
membrane-skins . . . epiphany . . .
my thought is fragments too. Just one more
violet pulse walled in by hammered stone.
He left without a word. Adept in disintegration,
confederate with each unknown cause,
a small foreign doctor in the autumn of a siege
watching a foreign painter die,
I put out fire with flashing wine.
Deep foreign ash fell in.

Lowlights

It took me some time to see
this isn't a girl. Head rams forward
to April's *Cosmopolitan*, strange
as prayer. His hands firm
bright pages as if they were wild.
One strip of Sellotape
flattens perforated plastic
to the nape, catching light.
Curled milky tufts nestle through,
baking to some kind of blonde.
The colourist in serious harem trousers
doesn't doubt her world. They share
their own warm alchemy. She checks
for stragglers. Five minutes more?
He nods. They know it all.
The turning fan scatters light
over rubber-gloved arms,
chrome flex from the drier,
the trolley – a tubular rainbow – of dye,
my Nescafé's zebra-gilt cup,
and over cutting mirrors everywhere:
vertical, double-sided, in ambush,
easily lost, out of place.

Unhoused
(for Kevin Andrews)

I wanted one glass tonight
of champagne, to your swim.
For having known you. But you'd laugh –

– no drink here without food
between six and nine. And bring
curd cheese from neighbours round the corner,
salad picked on hills, island liquor
you weren't supposed to touch.
'Half a glass,' you'd say, an impatient
accurate centaur, forgetting your pills.
'You come so seldom.' Only you knew
the dark padding loneliness. Your rough links,
copper spots of warmth in winter,
weighting like Agamemnon's gold
neckbone I never felt outside your house:
I couldn't afford them. Only a bracelet, a ring.

You'd know what to do with a neolithic axe
but what happened when lightning struck?
Those fits: I'd sit near, uselessly gentle.

The blue hands on your wall, meant
to keep off the eye – maybe they worked.
Who knows what might have happened?
How else could you go? Burnt scrub
on exposed Cithaeron that Easter
crackled with gods. You said, 'I like that –
crackling with gods.' We're born
to such hopeless houses,
strangers to what we love.

34

You shared what helped. The I Ching.
Dowland on pie-crust records. (I sent more –
they melted and warped in the mail.)
Goat-pipes. All your presences were real:

tangerine smoulder on a tripod,
books and the wood that held them,
iron tools on the plank by the stove.
Each had its history and smell.
When your grandchild was born
you twisted a bronze wire anchor.
I delivered it to the world
where you buried your gold.
The self you were goes into hiding
off Cythera, for God's sake, in a force
seven storm. Whatever happened,
there was that sweet smile after, floating back,
an assured child from an unshared reach.

Graffiti on Cactus and Cloud

No maps here. The sun, an apricot haze ,
tips cloudberry rays on Aigina's rim.
My bearings are the stone-pines' woodcut spikes
criss-crossing Salamis, island
of gold-flossed muddle in December pollution,
in a strait of too much history. They pierce
the Parthenon's grin. Reptilian clouds slide
over its bare nub, painting the temple out.

A marginal on an old doomed summit,
wind westerly, force five to seven,
I'm still friend of the threshold,
wolf-pelt and polished spear,
the gate-hinge closing at evening.

One cloud has written 'love'
in fine lombardic script on oatmeal sky.
Lights pepper the larger avenues.
I look down on the *Grande Bretagne*,
home of the brandy sour, Churchill's hold
in the civil war. Look back –
the writing's gone. Just the L's top:
you wouldn't guess there'd been a word there now.

Going down, the mountain rock is blued by neon ochre.
Saffron factory-flares from Eleusis
wave like mad hair. Colours don't change here,
only what makes them. My moonshadow strokes cactus
cut in daylight with a name I loved. The scar's grown

with the plant. I'll watch the ancient café wake.
Tiny tables welcome St Nicholas again,
guardian of millions through the diaspora.
Splotched respectable fingers sombrely tap roan marble.
A teaspoon falls. Old lips kiss rusty coffee.
Evening will be strange in the descent,
through the cacti's moonblue flesh
to air so differently dark.

After A-Level

Come early, he said. But going close
can you make black self-sufficient?
Is that what I'm going to do? Poisonously

in love, afraid, or out of touch,
you know the phone rang
while you were out. But life at home

has been not-feeling. The Tuscan scorpion
only got rid of by designer-spray,
and the porcupine, brought back

to the hills to keep down snakes,
doze at home on a random heap
of used durex under the pines.

I can deal with them. But virginity
and its loss? You'll hang there.
I remember looking up at black bees,

noisy, difficult grapes
in sugar-paper leaves,
the first time I'd seen olives.

Come early, he said, drunk.
He won't remember. Can nothing
change a black start?

PART TWO

Stepson

Snow on the scrapheap. Isolated lines
on which hope settles
suddenly apparent from the train:
body-shards related by one angle
to dead sky. Snow on the brickyard.
A sewage farm, silver linear.
Tawny pubic reeds blush through.
Black ice wriggles between.
Ghost-cranes stalk London docks:
diaspora of squeaking crystals.
Jake kneels between sphinx-paws
deciphering the east: the sea
this stolen obelisk traversed,
a smocking of snow hieroglyphs
against Embankment dusk. We walk back
on slipping fur, roan slush.
I crunch along, stumping and changing.

Watercourse

(i)

Our window is a drifting smoke
of rainlight in a cage of lichened thorn.
Pale grass, moor walls outside. Inside
there's Schubert song and coffee.
Marooned in Plato's geometric logic,
you sit by the fire,
a nineteenth-century charcoal sketch,
our daughter due in three months.

You are sealed and still.
The goldveined eye
of shifting embers,
river-sound of the piano
carrying a traveller's voice,
our curly dog nuzzling burrs
from her feet on the hearth:
only these move. The bull

who alarmed us yesterday
is a streaming statue
in the farther field.
We are each other's quiet
and concentration. No one
can reach us here.

Grass Wood. More rain. Dark afternoon.
We climb through shining parallelograms
of alder, buckthorn, wizened oak,
archaic mud and moss, black roots
and khaki stone. Scuts of rabbit vanish
on the diagonal, through splashing leaves.
A hedgehog climbs the path. 'How vulnerable,'
you say, stopping to watch the small
wet journey, remembering your other daughter,
teenaged and inaccessible. We carry this
with us everywhere, your *Winterreise*
of first love, false suns. Birthday cards
sent back unopened. One lost soul
behind a frozen thicket. 'So vulnerable,'
you say again, and turn away.
The hedgehog's gone. Only the ancient wood,
a sanctuary we can't diagnose, presses us,
glistening: a diver's cage of light.

Weekend Child

Salonika. The upper-city houses, oakleaf-grey,
heap down the slope. They stare like sick animals
depending on me for life. Ramparts echo.
Two women beat a rug on a rotting balcony
suspended over Turkish walls
(a rubbish dump). Two floral cats,
enormous crimson walruses,
undulate on purple cloth:
wealth displayed to the neighbourhood,
ikons of pride. This is the thump
of émigrés who'll never own their past,
on the back-end of a now-provincial city
revelling in ruin like a cat on heat.

Below, children play ball on St Sophia's front.
Their yellow sphere hangs, a moment,
on that famous lintel, fruit from another world.
But I can't stop thinking of our weekend child
as *he* goes back each Sunday. We watch him down his lane,
his small map of court-orders
and violent myth, a refugee
humping his BMX bag. What will he remember
from this time? The dog whines as he grows smaller
in lamplight between two worlds.

The Coffee-Icing Cow

As if a pewter glaze
had washed the black hollyhock
which thrust, one summer, high as my bed
in my parents' first joint house,
then dipped it in sunny coffee,
her skin is puddled silver-dun,
like a brown jade carving
you have to look at twice before you see.
She's a humpy chocolate rainbow
on the path between our houses,
in a water-meadow full
of head-high yellow flowers.
Summer hides rawness. For a moment I forget
the lurch into isolation of the winter fen,
this water-table rising and rising,
and the sad fire you aim at our new bed,
a Stone Age weaponry I cannot meet.

Scapegoats

The setting doesn't matter. Distance it
in antiquity if you like. Gold
anonymous bleakness, somewhere near Tiryns or Gla.
A jagged-seamed horizon, apt for sacrifice;
silver-grass olive-blades the only shade:
surreal snake-tongued stability of noon.

A dead hibiscus flower, furled like a squid,
moist as something cooked, sugar-glazed
and rotting, points our way – our procession
from the gate for the condemned. We carry god,
our offscouring, well-fettered with willow,
arbor infelix, the unproductive tree.

Beat him, if you like, with hissing squills.
Hear the flick of gristled withies,
the stripped-bark thump of fear.
One of us no longer, drugged against the end,
he's the dropped stitch in the universe,
a life the future won't count.

Grapes begin to stammer. Drums pulse
on the one-way road of his thought.
What glamorous squeak of blood
and psyche in reconstructed rites!
I've sat in seminars,
heard scholars talk as if it never happened now

while each weekend we feed our part-
time Mowgli who pushes back the light
we try to share. 'I like the dark,' and thwack!
on our green kitchen walls and cracking
stripped-pine table, a sudden self-annihilating
smallboy rage of bacchic drums.

Documents from lawyers he's never seen
dictate his visits here. Impotent as a raided bird,
he arrives with riddles of withholding
he doesn't understand. The stinging-nettle path,
interprets us – our colours, cooking, bank accounts –
in ways we never guess. He carries a jungle with him,

its furious black bees. Plus this trust,
the only gift he's got: that we can undergo
the rage he's learned, the rage he passes on.

Amniocentesis

Walled princess of the knot-garden
glinting with fat red fruit,
dependent from an amethyst-black shining plait,
you approach without modesty, native
from a vulnerable heartland,
spiralled round wayward seed,
hooks of peppergrain on white of softboiled egg.
I lived my physiology unthinkingly till now.

Your small lungs breathe inner liquid,
as the Greeks supposed we do.
You make your own antiquity in me.
Fireflies of premonition gather in my stem.
Thoughts of a burning spine,
starfall-silver gooseflesh in a winter labour ward,
a tambourine for ancient winds of pain . . .
I know your chemistry, at least.

That needle, a precision hummingbird,
sipped your round world. The doctor's
green apprentice interleaved your chromosomes
in glass. With an animal's determined privacy
you guard your ticking dark. Floating,
you prepare to wring my heart. One lightbulb
builds the bedroom round us.
How will you change our lives?

Daylilies glow on the path to the shed.
Will I be able to pause as you come,
if rocks are steep by the tough
furred flanks of the waterfall?
Imagination labours on into the night
to a last parapet, that neolithic fear
something will stay unlived.
A foreign drink rustles on the stove.

Foreigners

Last winter an exotic bird, mahogany, wall-eyed,
crested, invaded the community of mallards,
which the dog chases, not to catch,
but for that lift of wings to water,
the power of making things happen.
Three days the chestnut duck, surprised,
fed with the others, then was winged out
alone on the freezing bank. We had a sour,
snow-heaped winter. Huddled through white months
the ducks made silvery dented shades
on the edge, like mirrored nests.
But now, midsummer willow-fluff
spots the blue wind. A second family

of moor-chicks scatters among reed-roots.
I squelch where black water breeds
unseen. The stranger never returned.
Across the river, at the children's pool
you supervise your son. He splashes
the goggles we gave him last weekend.
Doesn't wave. Sometimes he says he's seen us
far off in the week. Me with the dog,
his father through the city in the car.
He pretends not to know or belong.
His loyalties move secretly
among each family's blind roots.
His quickness is not being seen.

Darwin's Great-great-great-granddaughter Smiles

Involuntary at first, they say –
a muscle-spasm, relaxation after wind –
this is smile from outer space, slowly engraving
individual, karma, race. It will end as courtesy's ghost
on quarried cheeks. A hundred years old,
your great-grandmother over the fen
responds to no pattern now but smile,
forgets the orchid she discovered,
the aquilegia named after her.

This minute change of face will draw you in
with the rest of us, to ambiguity.
Skeletons smile into earth while you
my winter daughter on a ruthless planet
struggle to make your new smile social.
Neurology sketches community's coin.
After this the meanings of smile
will not leave you alone.
It's a form of suffering too

and I, to whom you give this first
extraordinary signal, cannot guess
how you will use it. Who will be there
to undo it, say Yes, or misunderstand,
as I, growing separately older,
watch chalk and lemon leaves
flick over your ambiguous
no longer baby face
under tents of waving trees?

A Postcard to St Wite

'Please help our Ron with his moods
and let the children grow up safe.'
I didn't look further. That card
was top of a pile of prayers
in the saint's hole under her altar

where a fourteenth-century madman squeezed
for cure. What was it like in the pagoda
after the crowds had left
and only cloisters watched?
The church had a pilgrim's mouth, a shrine

for a desperate spring. We go back,
shopping. One tired woman wheels
a small grey pram. A man
unloading sacks of coffee
rests his back. I read, panicking, for news.

They will need to be cared for.
Our own baby's sleeping eyelids,
pale violet half-moons, already hide
what hurts to imagine.
Above, this green volcanic sky

disperses God knows what. Milk, meat, grass:
undeciphered, all over Europe,
like the lies and the motives for lies,
lethal atoms colonize the music
in a million children's bones.

Deus Absconditus

She has just discovered her feet
and learnt to rub her eyes when tired.
My ivory acrobat in repose, pale
bronze eyelashes, diligent petalled face.

The dog, in whom I have created too much love,
sleeps too, head along my knee,
and paws, on which the young snow shone,
extravagant in air.

'Tell her to grow quickly',
Nikos's letter says. 'Tell her
she has a friend in Crete. Teach her Greek
and when you come

I'll teach her to drink raki.'
What can I tell her, unknowing heir
to history's blind end? Here was a world
fit to communicate, richer for the devil in it

once. Islands' moral twilight . . .
letters fly between. You've been born
under an earthquake sky of ostrich feathers,
copper rust. We tread our hidden poison

day by day. My little threatened earth:
the aqueduct is choked and obsolete,
a curiosity behind the village
nobody goes to see. Unread,

the Phaistos disk waits in the museum,
identity's absent script. To place
so much in danger . . . One finger,
a half-inch long, is touching mine.

Playground

Gwen in the moat of Candax
delicately pours sand
quivering with cigarette butts
into a plastic fish.
The white peacock, dancer
in ruins of an Ottoman loo,
displays his phosphorescent fan.
Where the wall's thickest,
a Saracen mouth with crumpled teeth,
he drives his hen to the wire.

She offers Cretan crisps
to the oldest ibex
who bosses his stale flock
past a forty-foot Venetian redoubt.
Yellow creepers froth easily
over sandstone walls
two Sultans took twenty years
to penetrate. The hot sad fox
pads from his wooden tholos,
used to the crisps.

Seven small eagles whirr
unapproachable in the next cage.
Roundabouts turn. Children
are screamed at never to fall;
to come and eat cake. The flamingo,
a voluptuary with a Roman beak,
sips thick green water.
Gwen practises being butterfly.
A Cretan child whose words she doesn't know,
runs up, kisses and tweaks her:

'No! No! no! . . .' Three times her height,
grey vultures stand and stare.
We should have seen them circling
over Dikte. Siege, captivity, refusal,
history's skeletal flowers
in blue relentless light.
Loud silence of cicadas . . .
You grow so glad of night
under the walls of Candax
in the spring.

Reading Snow White *to my Daughter in Greek, Thinking of the Stepdaughter I Never See*

A woman looks out at snow. Cats watch her dream
of a name. Now a new woman looks in glass.
Here is a girl in red scrubbing floors,
smelling a rose, watched by the man on a horse.

She kneels to a man in the wood.
He leaves. Now she's alone. Owls, rabbits, deer
find her a cottage. Animals mean good,
or love. We don't see them dispose

of the stepmother in disguise,
who put the poison in the apple,
gave the apple to the girl:
this woman who looked only in glass.

What happened to the mother
who looked at the snow? I don't say
(you don't know this grammar yet)
how mothers and stepmothers change,

looking, and being looked at.
It takes a long time . . .
Sinister twinkling animals,
Hollywood ikons, modern Greek style:

a basket of images, poison at work
in the woodland no Cretan child
ever sees. Closer to home
I've seen a loved girl turn feral.

These pages lurk in the mind,
speak of your sister,
her mother, and me. Perhaps,
already, of you.

Visitors

They look for offerings, the residue
of worship. At lunch they talk of symbols.
All their books are gold.
Guides label these squat basins lustral,
these pillars aniconic. They hear,
but they're very hot. Pine trees buzz
with sparrows and cicadas. They revert
to nakedness in other people's world,
impressionist, their map of votive light.

Noon squashes the Hall of Axes,
filters vanilla and old rose
through the corrugated plastic
on the Ivory Acrobat's roof.
The Snake Goddess smiles to herself
in the shade of the midday daemon,
hour of emerald lizards, scorpions, wine.
We are asleep in the Kairatos Valley,
long haunch of an old ridge.

We talk of offerings, too. Perhaps we shouldn't try.
We've sent jewels in lacquer boxes,
an electronic typewriter, Beethoven Quartets,
vouchers for Miss Selfridge,
an ivory magnifying glass, a calculator,
books on archaeology, a Laura Ashley bag
and notes from a Harvard seminar on AIDS.
But your world-map won't admit us. You made
your brother bring your Christmas present back

in tears. You sold the camera. Do you look
at what you keep? We never know.
I watch your father wait. This is the land
he hoped you'd come to with us. Eighteen months old,
your pink mosquito-bitten sister plays
with dry snail-shells in the Throne Room's
soft flax dust and tackles the sadness of negatives.
So we believe. She knows nothing of you,
nor of excavation and its gentlemanly names.

Leper Island

(Spinalonga, an island off Crete, fortified by Venice and later inhabited by Turkish smugglers, became Europe's last leper colony in 1903. The lepers were incarcerated there by force. They used the ruined fort-buildings to make a community, which they were forced to disband in 1956. Leprosy, they say, came to Europe with the returning Crusaders)

We read directions in our skin's
crossed stars. Laundry tubs,
the fumigation bell, carnations
in a porcelain WC: there is precision here
if I could see it. I can't hand you
meaning on a stem, snailtrack nodules
on a fore-arm I can't feel. All I can do
is play with the failing light

here on this boat with this child,
this blue. That once-simple act
of love: there were important things
to feel if I had known. Unforgivable
incubation, an atlas of sea-ice,
absorption of the bone: how could I tell,
at first? Here's our fortress of amputation
under castellation and the lion of St Mark.

Look! our re-usable cemetery,
disinfection-room, and charnel-house.
The graffiti read 'Avenue of Pain'.
'To Golgotha'. Here was our newspaper,
The Satirist. And our theatre:
we invite the mainland mayor.

My brother walked down the mountain,
God's forehead to His mouth

(over the water you can see His face).
He found a mule's graveyard.
Coloured tails, cracked skins,
and grey bones, fossils, free.
I remember the hills. They shipped us
to ourselves in straitjackets.
Here the pain shows simple.
We discount it. No one dies alone.

The mainland government
allows us to marry,
ships the babies away to be safe.
There are more of us than you know.
We're in your blood.
Our dead-end island came
from your crusades of love.
We don't want to leave it now.

South Wind

Where does darkness come from?
Mad red glare of the horse-fly
under the cliff, fangs
of the chocolate stoat,
anger of seven eagles in the filthy zoo,

slimy red bathroom tiles at night
and a poisonous millipede
beside the baby's boat.
Wind rages through church bells
above our bed. It drags an iron grate

across the roof. These solitary
horrors from jungle floors
will run through melting factories
when our own dark comes true.
A plundered faked-up palace rests

above us – house of ponderous myth
for a million foreigners each year,
shattered on a day in spring
when the wind blew from the south.
We know this from fire-signs,

black stones, cracked columns,
melted gypsum in seven chemical forms:
destruction levels. Those burnt floors
pack a Sleeping Beauty world,
ceramic deaths, arms stretching out

to catch. The baby learns to climb
on its theatral steps. At night I read.
Egyptians on their safe papyrus
complained – you could call it mourning –
at the time. 'What shall *we* do

for cedar for our mummies?
Our nobles were embalmed
with what the foreigners brought.
With oil from as far away as Keftiu.
But now they come no more.'

Stinging Libyan red sand
blasts our house from the south.
I go back to bed
quietly, not waking the baby
who sleeps through the wind.

Orgeat

He was full of anger.
A bad combination, Welsh and Cypriot
working for English. Ready to dislike
(I'd heard so much against),
I was unprepared for his passion,
the way he took religion,
what people really might have felt or done,
demonically. Desperate to disprove
the summit-shrines *were* shrines –
just, he said, a dance
of the élitist European mind –
he climbed every peak on the island.
Egrets hunt frogs through fallen doorways,
bee-eaters endure unseasonable rain
on wire by a purple road,
and he climbed mountains, when he could.
Everyone moves more easily
through other people's distances and gods.

On the tallest he met a man
with a sack of snow
for the ancient drink, relic
(though you can't say so)
of Turkish taste and government.
The August festival was near.
They needed quince, almond-water,
orange-water, snow. He expected
to disprove sanctuary. Instead
he found a secret well,
summer snow deep in the mountain,
Ida's wrinkle of white dark,
and memories of how to cool the dance.

Tempers and knives are hot up there
on summer nights among the feuds
and yellow dresses, determined flowers
who know they've only got this little time
to bloom. He also taught Kung Fu,
a special kind, to Heraklion skinheads
on the Villa roof.

Yew Berries

At my wedding he came over the grass
cupping them, drunk. 'Did you know
the thrill in your garden,
safe if you spit out the seed?
It's the flesh . . .' I half-thought
of Agatha Christie and taxine
but barely noticed. Why do I think of it now?
Did I dream a party at his place
years ago? A small brown bottle
in the bathroom, like (I now imagine)
what Romeo got hold of,
meant to make orgasm last:
'But it's lethal. A drop too much
and you're gone.' Red, promising,
my parents' sunny garden, a wedding.
Safe if you spit out the seed.
Why do I think of that now?

PART THREE

Builders

I meet them in cycles
    in houses I inhabit, paint,
        and leave. They sit in my dusty futures,
            tired – Colin, Rodney, Steve,

talking of homes they'll build
    for themselves one day.
        They are ruthless of course.
            A danger to marriage, creepers,

bare feet, patience, dogs.
    They gassed the house last week.
        But I like the way they change
            how you see, so casually

and for ever. They speak of resting –
    of sockets, skirting-boards and living-space –
        with assurance and tough hands.
            Then they move on. I find them later
                in an unforeseeable place.

Priest's Child

I come from a house of understanding
full of paintings I don't like
and panicky unwritten rules whose basic rule
is what you mustn't understand
but everything's a sign of something else.
Is there life beyond unravelling the bowels?
Will I in turn pass overdrawn signs
and their hurt ways of seeing, to a child?

It was no good knowing words.
Romans will come with straight lines,
leprosy, Egyptian cats, new traffic-ways
and water tax, their capacity for being unaware,
for making us pay to vote.
They'll relieve us of understanding
and put everything outside to dry.

I can see tired excited fishermen far off,
puzzled, dazzled – something political –
following a prisoner beyond a crowd
up a small red slope of olives
– smaller, more tortured trunks than these –
because something is written, letters I can't read,
and they must follow, however eccentric and shabby.
Afterwards they'll meet again and say

'Did our hearts not burn within us on the road?'
I'm tired of piecing everything
together from scratch, god's script
on the liver at death, redwing and rockthrush
on the left, the deft politician's sneeze.
I've done all this. But there's been
no one to see or share how.

These stones, tearing last year's nets
under the olives, shout with signs,
but I won't show you now.
It's dark. Romans, as I told you, will occur
to invent cement, cosmetic glass,
the urban slum, reform and chequered brick.
There's one door left, black on black.
Am I coming in or going out?

Incubus

(Responses to the play A Mouthful of Birds, *by Caryl Churchill and David Lan, which sketched lives violently changed by madness in 1980s Britain and in Euripides' play* The Bacchae)*

(i)
Dionysus

Something has stopped, touched.
I let her go. Coffeebreak
for prison officers. *I've got*
to look after someone.
Smiling that goes on smiling
in the dark. She who releases
is bound.

Laughter in empty provinces.
Exit. Ankles bloom
in red fanned ribs.
The moon grows downward, frantic.
Marble cocktail parties,
egg that broke in a handbag.
The dogstar howls behind glass.

I loved this city.
Take it, then: a fat black map,
lettering of negatives,
talk that went nowhere,
Volvo that crashed on the Ring Road.
A cynical godhead in frills.
swings from your door.

(ii)
Transvesta

So many petticoat nightmares
of trivial shame. Her boiler-suit
winks from the suitcase, a hidden
and halted joy, shoved in the cupboard
as soon as it's over.
Rival candidates at interview
in the five o'clock waiting-room.
Work on the railway . . . We celebrate
endurance of secrets separately.
Red jumps on the back of white. Kitchen units
mask a rising sump of desperation.
Pearling windows breathe zinc.
The baby claps her hands.

(iii)
Recidivist

Dry spangles . . . a virus in cells . . .
I loved it . . . work in the blood.
Expense account . . . god of the staircase . . .
Profits . . . Roll the carpet back
for evening karate. Gilt shoes, gloss paint
and stinging genitals. *I'm still afraid.*
And at hazard, unemployed.
Gin bottles behind borrowed paperbacks,

bulimia in other people's kitchens,
the raided freezer. *Not going
to the meeting tonight?*
Flaked from her shell by a mother's
inaccurate regard. Black suns . . .
She stares into a house of crimson rain.

(iv)
Holidays

Skies not alien enough.
The villa that went wrong.
Cabbage-whites on the nuclear dump,
nightclub behind the glamorous ancient site.
Something wouldn't sleep. Schist
glints in the marriage-fissure.
Diffidently, transposed in daylight,
a long-rejected parent dissects the child.
Consecrated bedsits of the heart . . .
When you're not thinking,
That's when the nightmares start.
She didn't expect that clumsy kitchen,
rigged gas-meters, rain,
or a tassel of coal-dust meat-flies
– that bulk of buzzing soot
on the thyrsus of valerian –
between her and the vicious main road.

(v)
Pentheus

Blood breaks from the teapot.
Pale hands, torn zip
but free. With syrup, violence,
roses and obsession, Cybele smiles
in the mirror of the tenement loo.

*

Dry rustles invade the window,
dogfox-plunder, hurt by a word:
You think it won't happen to you.
Lace on male muscles! look! a theatre in the home!
Judas-branches fleck the upstairs hall.

*

Why glamorise madness?
The blackbird goes alone.
Drab victims dismembered to music . . .
a torso . . . *No one will doubt* . . . To the clinic . . .
violation . . . virus . . . and such shame.

(vi)
Breakthrough

A mouthful of lives in chipboard
makeshift rooms. The backroom voodooist,
the neighbour who came to beg with yellow eyes,
the public-library ventriloquist
who lost someone else's voice
in disguise as herself. Histories
of the sulphur planet. Compulsions creep
from the eye where the fire should be.

Red Admirals scatter in the playground
by the Body Repair Works on our industrial estate.
How can you know what's safe?
Tesserae of maternal days.
Shopping and pushchairs and rain.
A chasm where the Sibyl died convulsed.
How can I get there? Redshift.
Love in green sandals. Fury on spotted cement.

Or exchange of body-fluids, the carnal carriage-way,
black as the weeping rock gods swore by. Breath stops
under hydrangeas in a northern suburb.
Flute is the sound of freedom, the unencumbered soul.
Lorries . . . balance . . . grief on skidding wheels.
The chariot skirls on mud, rattles
a dead heroic father's naked feet.
His thinning hair feathers our road.

Jazz Class

She has a lion waiting,
leapfrogs, back to mirror,
doing the opposite as always,
in tights and an Oxfam jumper,
surrounded by satin leotards.
Tongue out, as if that helped
to learn svelte, five-year-old poise.
She's only three. Asked
what they're doing, swinging
twelve-inch hips, they say,
'Michael Jackson dancing.' Or,
'Being grown-up.' Other kids, older,
brought *My Little Pony*, a clutch
of Barbie Dolls. He's a shadow
of cinnamon mud in the mirror-wall.
She moves as if his eyes could touch.
Is he supposed to be lonely?
Girls should fly like fairies,
the boy march like a soldier.
But he won't. The Body-Centre leader
tries to make him swagger like a man
alone. Suddenly everyone's told
to kiss goodbye. Lion to shoulder,
she forgets. Afterwards tells me
she liked the jumping best.

Royal Road

Icicles explode on a Space Invaders screen
in an English pub. She's looking back
over gin and French, a baby on her arm,
remembering another earth

not what she lives now:
a scrum of jewel-ridden dust,
blistered moonstone sky,
sunsets of malachite and shrilling frogs.

Scrabbling through hot corridors
to leaning Ali Baba jars, on a hill
once called Kefala, Europe's labyrinthine vulva
on the medieval map, she found black teacups,

thin as a breath, The Captain of the Blacks,
The Lily Prince. To speak
of the destruction of cities,
bleached childhood, hot T-shirts and lemonade,

Arabic vine-roots, ceremonies of giving
without disapproval, Greek words disinterred
like starfish in the soil:
you can't remake what's gone.

'What does "Is" Mean?'

That we may have to share two rooms in town
and leave not just Daddy but the dog.

For the shaggy garden,
where you're Papageno in duck boots,

there'll be people. 'I don't want people.'
You will. I hope you will.

And I need them. We'll be near theatres,
playgrounds, friends. 'They're not my friends.'

They're not all mine yet either but we'll find . . .
Well, you won't stifle in this town, you see.

We'll be away.' 'I like our house.
Our front garden has gates.

Our walls are white like the school.
My window looks on sunrise when it's day.'

In the Distance

If after all this I can't love
or can't love you
is it you or I at fault?
A rash on my throat,
our new shadowed garden,
building and fencing and paint.
While you're away the baby wakes
each night. After settling her
I cannot sleep for sadness.
Perhaps I really can't care
for any movement of your mind or self
except for pity, which you'd hate.
But that's not right.
Our dead trees wait for winter.
The past invades. Our bedroom's
the same layout as another years ago,
with a round white paper shade,
a palm and balsam poplar
up outside. That blowing linen curtain,
bricked-off suburb of a town you hardly know,
crops up in this strange storage,
mad awkward house, impossible wallpaper
we'll have to change.